PISTOL CITY

Pilot

Deshon Smith

dizzyemupublishing.com

DIZZY EMU PUBLISHING

1714 N McCadden Place, Hollywood, Los Angeles 90028

dizzyemupublishing.com

PISTOL CITY
Pilot
Deshon Smith

This edition first published in the United States
in 2023 by Dizzy Emu Publishing

dizzyemupublishing.com

PISTOL CITY

Pilot

Deshon Smith

<u>PISTOL CITY</u>

<u>Pilot</u>

Based on True Events!

Written by

Deshon S. Smith

<u>TEASER</u>

                                        FADE IN:

EXT. HIDDEN FOOT PATH - NIGHT

Wearing a **SKI-MASK**(Shiesty) under a hoodie. KISHEED WATSON,
17, very tall, slim, walks behind some run down, single
family apartments.

In the background - BP Gas Station. Better known as the
"Corner Store." Overgrown bushes camouflage its Green and
Yellow sign from drivers coming off the highway into town.

EXT. 25 SHENSTONE LANE - SAME TIME

Sporting an **Afro** with small curls. TAEKWON JORDAN, 17, very
tall, slim, walks down a drive way, pass ground lights that
display a well manicured lawn.

In the background - The Jordan's house. 2856 square feet, 5
beds, 2.5 baths property. Custom in-ground pool, privacy
fence, topped off with a full size basketball court.

EXT. HIDDEN FOOT PATH - NIGHT

KIsheed's POV. The back of the run down apartments are
sporadically placed every 10 feet. Suddenly, we hear a
commotion. SCREAMS! A car door slams.

INT. CUSTOMIZED DODGE CHARGER SCATPACK - SAME TIME

Taekwon places his cellphone into a holder attached to the
windshield. Types on the screen.

<u>Cellphone Screen</u>: Directions - Norfolk State University
Spartan Suites. 2hr 53min (186.0 mi)

Taekwon starts the Scatpack, latches the seatbelt, and
slowly backs out of the driveway.

                         CELLPHONE
              Head north on Shenstone lane.

EXT. HIDDEN FOOT PATH - NIGHT

The foot path abruptly ends and Kisheed arrives at Dale
Homes Apartments in Portsmouth, Virginia.

It's DARK, except for a dim street light, FlIcKeRiNG in
front of a metal picket fence. *quietly* he jumps it.
BLLLAATTT! A car drives-by. Unloads an automatic weapon.

Kisheed slams up against the nearest apartment. A/C unit on
his right. Window to the left. Kisheed gently pries it open.
Climbs into the room. After fumbling around in the dark.

Turns on a small lamp.

INT. DALE HOMES APARTMENTS - KISHEED'S BEDROOM - CONTINUOUS

Anthony Edwards, Sha'carri Richardson, LaMelo Ball, Megan
the Stallion, Allen Iverson, posters litter the wall.

A crumpled up honor roll certificate completes the montage
as proof. "Hard work beats talent when talent doesn't work
hard."

Furnished on a wooden dresser: Basketball trophies draped
with championship medals. 3D Printer. PRINTING. And a folded
Dorian Finney-Smith XL Jersey.

Mounted to the back of the door - Plastic Nerf basketball
goal. "*Black Lives Matter*" and DO NOT ENTER stickers wrap up
the front. Directly on the floor rest a queen size bed.

Kisheed sits down. Turns on the TV. WT-KR News 3. News
Reporter: In sports - Taekwon Jordan. Top ten basketball
recruit in the country. Commits to Norfolk State University.

Kisheed picks up his cellphone. Types on the screen. ALARM -
10:30 p.m. He turns off the lamp, lays down, and pulls the
cover on top.

EXT. US 58 EAST - NIGHT

The Customized Dodge Charger ScatPack travels in the middle
of a 3-lane highway. In the fast lane a DARK GREEN
CHALLENGER with Florida plates SHRIEKS pass.

INT. CUSTOMIZED DODGE CHARGER SCATPACK - CONTINUOUS

MUSIC CUE: "ScatPacc" By Baby Hot X & NLE Choppa.

Taekwon flicks the high beams. Dark green challenger's brake
lights illuminate. It slows down until they are side by
side. Dashboard - Speedometer 50mph.

HONK! HONK! HONK! Taekwon stomps the gas. Dark green
challenger does the same. VRRROOOMMM! Dashboard -
Speedometer 63mph, 78mph, 89mph...

INT. DALE HOMES APARTMENTS - LIVING ROOM - NIGHT

Kisheed sits on a foldable chair next to MARQUAIL, 18,
paraplegic, in front of a 60 inch flat screen. They play NBA
2K on a PlayStation 5 gaming system.

                    KISHEED
          Y'all remember when I use to dunk
          on niggas like this?

Kisheed presses a button on the controller.

On TV Screen: Lebron James dunks on Draymond Green.

Marquail moves the left analog stick around, stops, and does
the same.

                    MARQUAIL
          Yeah, and I remember you gettin'
          dropped off just like this. CURRY!

On TV Screen: James Wiseman takes the ball out of bounds,
passes it to Curry. Chef shoots it from the logo. SWISH!

                    KISHEED
          Yo... That's cap! When?

                    MARQUAIL
          That night at the rec invitational
          tournament. Buddy, had you lookin'
          crazy. I couldn't do nothin' but
          laugh.

                    KISHEED
          We still won tho. And why you
          bringin' up old stuff?

                    MARQUAIL
          That's you! Mister, I'm goin' to
          play in the NBA one day.

                    KISHEED
          My boy, if I didn't drop out of
          high school. I would be in the
          league right now!

Behind Kisheed and Marquail - A coffee table with backwoods wrappers, an ashtray, shot glasses, half empty Hennessy bottle, and small clear bags of marijuana.

INT. DALE HOMES APARTMENTS - CONTINUOUS

On the couch - KATORAH, 22, beautiful, light skin, ball cap covering long braids, identifies as a stud, takes a pull off a blunt lodged between her fingers.

                    KATORAH
               (coughs)
          Bro, that's cap! You can't play in
          the NBA at seventeen. You have to
          be nineteen. Or go to college for
          at least one year.

                    KISHEED
          What about Jalen Duren? He was
          eighteen.

                    KATORAH
          Yeah, but he didn't play in the NBA
          until he was nineteen years old.

Next to Katorah - DIEUSON, pronounced /die-u-son/, 21, linebacker build, sips on a red plastic cup filled with brown liquor.

Dieuson gives Katorah the Shannon Sharpe viral meme look.

                    DIEUSON
               (sarcastically)
          How do you know? Katorah!

                    KATORAH
          Because, I'm not dumb. Like you,
          Dieuson!

Marquail and Kisheed laugh.

                    DIEUSON
          Oh, you got jokes.

Dieuson scoots a little bit closer to Katorah. SNATCH! He rips off her ball cap.

                    KATORAH
          Bro, what the fuck are you doin'?

                    DIEUSON
          Gimme that shit.

Katorah reaches for the hat but Dieuson quickly moves it.

                         DIEUSON (cont'd)
               Ha-ha. Too slow.

Katorah stands up, lifts her shirt, BRANDISHING a pistol.

                         KATORAH
               Bro, give me back my motherfuckin'
               hat.

Dieuson rises like DEEBO from the movie "Friday." Gets right
up into Katorah's grill.

                         DIEUSON
               Or what?

                         KATORAH
               Or I'm gonna slime yo fugly ass!

                         KISHEED
               Yo... Y'all chill out.

In the blink of an eye - Dieuson bear hugs Katorah. Body
slams her on the couch. He climbs on top, pins her wrist
down, then passionately grinds his zipper on hers.

Dieuson goes in for a kiss. Katorah turns and SCREAMS!

                         KATORAH
               GET OFF OF ME!

Dieuson moves Katorah's hands until they are at the top of
her head. Forces both of her wrist into the palm of his
right hand. Uses his left hand to squeeze Katorah's breast.

                         KATORAH (cont'd)
               STOP, DIEUSON!

Fed up, Kisheed SLAMS the controller down. Makes his way
over to the couch. Pulls the coffee table back. Strenuously
tugs Dieuson backwards.

Dieuson flops on the floor. Katorah pushes Kisheed out of
the way. Yanks out the pistol, cocks it, points it at
Dieuson.

                         KATORAH (cont'd)
               BRO, YOU GOT ME FUCKED UP!

           KISHEED   MARQUAIL
       CHILL!!!   KATORAH!!!

<u>ACT ONE</u>

EXT. INTERSTATE 264 - SAME TIME

A highway sign illuminates.

<u>Digital Highway Sign</u>: Berkeley bridge opening in progress.

INT. CUSTOMIZED DODGE CHARGER SCATPACK - CONTINUOUS

                    CELLPHONE
          There's a backup ahead. Causing a
          twenty minute delay. I've found an
          alternate route. Eight minutes
          faster.

<u>Cellphone Screen</u>: Alternate Route - PROMPT.

Taekwon presses the screen.

                    CELLPHONE (cont'd)
          You're on the fastest route. You
          should reach your destination by
          eleven thirteen p.m.

Taekwon takes the Frederick blvd exit. Makes a left at the
light. Turns right onto Turnpike road.

Taekwon follows Turnpike until a thick cloud of white smoke
makes it nearly impossible to see anything beyond the
headlights.

Consequently, he slows down. Creeps closer... closer...
Until he reaches a large crowd of people standing in the
middle of the street.

Directly under a bridge. With cars parked on both sides.

EXT. UNDER BRIDGE - CONTINUOUS

A BYSTANDER, early 20s, standing in the middle acknowledges
him.

                    BYSTANDER
                 (to the crowd)
          Watch out! Watch out! Another scat
          is tryin' to get in.

The crowd opens up to REVEAL: a CAR burning rubber, doing
donuts, driving recklessly in a circle.

A few BRAVE SOULS try to dodge the vehicle. OTHER BYSTANDERS scream with excitement.

                    BYSTANDER #2   BYSTANDER #3
Yeaaahhh!!!   Woooo-hoooo!!!

The REST have their cellphones out recording the live footage.

                         BYSTANDER #4
               We live!!!

EXT. UNDER BRIDGE - CONTINUOUS

Taekwon enters. Revs the engine - VROOM, VROOM. Puts his left foot on the brake pedal. SMASH! Floors the accelerator.

The supercharger lets out a high pitched wine. Exhaust rumbles, then pops. Tires screech. VROOOMMM!

The Customized Dodge Charger ScatPack spins in a circle.

                         CELLPHONE
               Make a U-turn. Head east on
               Turnpike road. Make a U-turn.
               Follow constitution avenue...

INT. DALE HOMES APARTMENTS - LIVING ROOM - NIGHT

Kisheed grabs Katorah's hands. Pushes the gun down until it's pointed at the floor.

                         KISHEED
               Calm down Katorah!

Katorah tucks the pistol back into her waistband.

                         DIEUSON
               Relax Katorah. I was just playin'
               with you.

Dieuson grabs the ball cap. Holds it in the air.

                         DIEUSON (cont'd)
               Here, take your stupid hat.

Katorah snatches the cap. Drapes it back over her braids. Katorah sits down with a different look in her eye.

                         KISHEED
               Y'all wylin'!

                    KATORAH
          That's yo boy.

                    DIEUSON
          That's you.

                    KISHEED
          Everybody just relax. C'mon y'all
          take a shot.

Kisheed grabs the Hennessy bottle, pours, and hands them
out. CLINK! They guzzle them down.

                    MARQUAIL
          Ayo, Sheed. Can you take me to the
          crib?

                    KISHEED
          Yeah, I got you.

Kisheed opens the door. Pushes Marquail outside.

                    KISHEED (cont'd)
          Yo... I'm about to roll this nigga
          home. Y'all Gucci?

                    DIEUSON
          I'm good.

                    KATORAH
          I'm Gucci.

Kisheed gives them a serious look.

                    KISHEED
          Aight, don't fuck up my crib. I'll
          be right back!

EXT. UNDER BRIDGE - NIGHT

The crowd re-opens. VROOM! VROOM! The Customized Dodge
Charger ScatPack exits.

INT. CUSTOMIZED DODGE CHARGER SCATPACK - CONTINUOUS

                    CELLPHONE
          Head west on Turnpike road.

Cellphone Screen: Directions - Turn left on Frederick Blvd.
Then slight right. Take Interstate 264 exit towards Norfolk.

Taekwon shakes his head.

                    TAEKWON (V.O.)
          Right back where I started.

EXT. DALE HOMES APARTMENTS - NIGHT

Kisheed expeditiously pushes Marquail's wheelchair.

                    MARQUAIL
          That shit was crazy, right?

                    KISHEED
          Right! And it got me to thinkin'.

                    MARQUAIL
          About what?

                    KISHEED
          Everything! I really need to get my
          shit together before the same thing
          happens to me.

                    MARQUAIL
          So what you gonna do?

                    KISHEED
          Ima just focus on tryin' to get
          into the league.

                    MARQUAIL
          But accordin' to Katorah you have
          to be nineteen or go to college.

                    KISHEED
          Yeah, I know. But, I don't have
          time to waste. It's now or never.

Kisheed thinks for a moment.

                    KISHEED (cont'd)
          If there was some way I could get
          in front of a college basketball
          coach. I would be Gucci.

                    MARQUAIL
          At what? Gettin' dropped off?

Kisheed chuckles.

                    KISHEED
          Yeah right.

... Kisheed stops in front of a silver ramp, with two metal rails and black non-skid tape strips attached at the bottom.

                    KISHEED (cont'd)
          Aight, Ima holla at you!

Kisheed walks in the opposite direction of his apartment.

                    MARQUAIL
          Ayo, where you goin'?

                    KISHEED
          To the corner store. To get a soda
          and sum chips.

                    MARQUAIL
          Bruh, take off that damn shiesty.

                    KISHEED
          Hell nah, my opps might be out.

EXT. TURNPIKE ROAD/FREDERICK BLVD - INTERSECTION - NIGHT

Green Clean Express Auto Wash, CVS, Dunkin Donuts, and Starbucks. Congest the four-way intersection. The Customized Dodge Charger ScatPack stops in the left turn lane.

INT. CUSTOMIZED DODGE CHARGER SCATPACK - CONTINUOUS

The Dashboard Illuminates: "Low Fuel." The traffic light turns green. Taekwon turns left. Drives pass the exit.

                    CELLPHONE
          Make a U-Turn at Deep creek
          Boulevard...

EXT. BP GAS STATION - FREDERICK BLVD - MOMENTS LATER

Taekwon parks next to a gas pump. Exits. Takes out his wallet, removes a debit card, slides it into the slot, and patiently waits.

In his *peripheral,* notices a dark shadow walking towards him. Glances at the person. Drops the wallet. SKRT! Taekwon takes off running.

                    KISHEED
                 (to Taekwon)
          Yo...

Kisheed walks up with cellphone in hand.

                         KISHEED (V.O.)
            Damn, I was just gonna ask him if I
            could snap a pic of his scat.

Kisheed picks up the wallet. Looks inside the car. To
REVEAL: KEYS are in the ignition, cellphone cradled in a
holder connected to the windshield.

Kisheed steps back. Stares at the car as if he has an *Angel*
on one shoulder and a *Devil* on the other.

                         KISHEED (V.O.) (cont'd)
            You only live once.

Kisheed jumps inside the Customized Dodge Charger ScatPack.
"SKIRTS OFF."

EXT. FREDERICK BLVD - NIGHT

Taekwon runs full speed until he reaches a church. Tries
opening the door. LOCKED! Sprints behind and hides.

... Taekwon looks around. Then makes a dash for the road.
Flags down a small pickup truck.

                         TAEKWON
            Help! Help! Help me!!!

A MOTORIST, early 60s, pulls over to the side of the road.
Rolls down the passenger's window.

                         MOTORIST
            You need a ride buddy?

                         TAEKWON
            No, I was just carjacked! Can you
            call nine one one for me?

                         MOTORIST
            No problem.

INT. DALE HOMES APARTMENTS - LIVING ROOM - NIGHT

Video game controllers are on the floor. Couch pushed
against the wall. The coffee table still out of place with
the various items on top.

TIFANY SAVAGE, 34, vulgar, blunt, foul mouth, enters.

                    TIFANY
          Look at my damn house.

Tifany walks down the hallway to Kisheed's bedroom. Opens
the door, turns on the light.

PRE-LAP: Passionate moans.

INT. DALE HOMES APARTMENTS - KISHEED'S BEDROOM - CONTINUOUS

SMACK, SMACK, SMACK! Dieuson holds Katorah by the waist
side. He pounds inside her.

                    TIFANY
          KISHEED!

                    DIEUSON
               (screams)
          AHHH!

Dieuson quickly pulls up his pants.

                    KATORAH
          OH MY GOD!

Katorah grabs Kisheed's jersey. Covers herself.

                    TIFANY
          Y'all get the fuck out of here with
          that shit!

INT. CUSTOMIZED DODGE CHARGER SCATPACK - NIGHT

MUSIC CUE: "Shiesty Summer" by Pooh Shiesty.

On the center console. Kisheed's cellphone illuminates "MA."
Kisheed turns the radio down to the lowest level.

                    KISHEED
          Hello?

                    TIFANY (O.C.)
          Where you at?

                    KISHEED
          Ummm... At Marquail's house.

                    TIFANY (O.C.)
          Well, I hope you're planning on
          spending the night. Because I told
                    (MORE)

                         TIFANY (O.C.) (cont'd)
                    you. If you not in my house by
                    midnight. Don't come home.

CLICK! Tifany hangs up.

Kisheed peeps into the rear view mirror. A COP CAR trails
behind. Kisheed takes the next turn into a closed Rite Aid
turned Advance Auto Parts.

The cop car follows. Turns on the police lights. Kisheed
stops. Shifts the gear lever into manual mode. Gently revs
the engine - vroom, vroom.

Without warning -- Kisheed stomps the accelerator. Skirts
pass Advance Auto Parts onto a side road.

OFFICER JOHNSON, African American, early 30s, and OFFICER
GAMBLE, early 40s, pursue in separate police cruisers.

The Customized Dodge Charger ScatPack explodes through the
streets of Portsmouth. With speeds reaching over 100 mph.

"Low Fuel." chimes consistently.

Ahead: Airline, Portsmouth, Missy Elliott Boulevard,
intersection.

Officer Gamble speeds up. Positions the vehicle along the
rear quarter panel. Cranks the wheel. WHHAAAAMM!

The Customized Dodge Charger ScatPack spins violently out of
control, flips, and ejects Kisheed through the driver's side
window.

SMACK! Suddenly Kisheed snaps back to reality.

INT. CUSTOMIZED DODGE CHARGER SCAT PACK - NIGHT

Without warning -- Another police cruiser pulls in from
behind the first. It positions so that Kisheed won't be able
to "Skirt off."

Kisheed shifts the car into park. Tucks his Shiesty in
between the seat. Grabs Taekwon's wallet.

EXT. ADVANCE AUTO PARTS - CONTINUOUS

Officer Johnson and Officer Gamble exit their vehicles with
flash lights in hand. They walk to the back of the vehicle.
Shine their lights on the rear fender and tires.

Officer Johnson walks to the driver's side door. Officer Gamble walks to the passenger's. Kisheed rolls down the window.

                    OFFICER JOHNSON
          Do you know why we pulled you over?

Kisheed speaks with a *nervous* tone.

                    KISHEED
          No, sir!

                    OFFICER JOHNSON
          We've been receiving a bunch of
          calls about cars driving recklessly
          in this neighborhood.

                    KISHEED
          That wasn't me, because I just left
          the gas station. Sir!

                    OFFICER JOHNSON
          License and registration!

Kisheed pulls out Taekwon's drivers license. Hesitantly, focuses on the glove box.

                    KISHEED
          Here you go. Sorry, I don't have
          the registration.

Officer Johnson confiscates the license. Retreats to his police cruiser. Officer Gamble follows.

INT./EXT. OFFICER JOHNSON'S POLICE CRUISER - CONTINUOUS

Officer Johnson rolls down the window. Takes a close look at the license. Then types on a laptop.

                    OFFICER JOHNSON
          Jim, have you been keeping up with
          the news?

                    OFFICER GAMBLE
          Yes, I watch it everyday.

                    OFFICER JOHNSON
          Did you hear about that top ten
          college basketball player? Taekwon
          Jordan.

                    OFFICER GAMBLE
          The boy from North Carolina? Who
          committed to Norfolk State when he
          could've went to Duke or Kentucky.

                    OFFICER JOHNSON
          Exactly! Check this out.

Officer Johnson hands him the identification.

                    OFFICER GAMBLE
          Taekwon Jordan? No way! Let me go
          check.

INT. CUSTOMIZED DODGE CHARGER SCATPACK - CONTINUOUS

Kisheed peels a social security card out of Taekwon's
wallet. A closer look REVEALS: Taekwon Jordan 453-21-6454.

                    KISHEED
          Oh, shit! This Taekwon Jordan's
          car.

At the drivers window - Officer Gamble shines the flashlight
on the license then on Kisheed.

                    OFFICER GAMBLE
          Taekwon Jordan?

                    KISHEED
          Y-e-ah.

                    OFFICER GAMBLE
          Step out of the vehicle please!

EXT. CUSTOMIZED DODGE CHARGER SCAT PACK - CONTINUOUS

Officer Gamble shines the flashlight on Kisheed.

                    OFFICER GAMBLE
          How tall are you?

                    KISHEED
          Six foot six.

                    OFFICER GAMBLE
          Top ten college basketball player
          in the country. What are you doing
          in the most dangerous city in
          Virginia?

                    KISHEED
          I was gettin' some gas.

                    OFFICER GAMBLE
          Alright, you can get back in.

INT./EXT. OFFICER JOHNSON'S POLICE CRUISER - CONTINUOUS

Officer Gamble returns. Hands Officer Johnson the ID.

                    OFFICER GAMBLE
          It's definitely him.

                    OFFICER JOHNSON
          Wow, we need to get him to the
          university before he gets into
          trouble.

They lock eyes, nod, then BLURT out:

          OFFICER GAMBLE   OFFICER JOHNSON
     Police escort!   Police escort!

                    OFFICER GAMBLE
          I'll lead and you follow.

                    OFFICER JOHNSON
          Ten-four! I'll call Norfolk state
          police department and let them know
          we're on the way.

INT. CUSTOMIZED DODGE CHARGER SCAT PACK - CONTINUOUS

Kisheed nervously stares into the driver's side mirror.
Officer Gamble walks into view. Leans down to the open
window.

                    OFFICER GAMBLE
          You're in luck Taekwon. We're going
          to give you a police escort to
          Norfolk State.

                    KISHEED
          W-h-at?

                    OFFICER GAMBLE
          We're not going to let anything
          happen to you in our city.

EXT. OFFICER JOHNSON'S POLICE CRUISER - CONTINUOUS

Officer Johnson walks to the Customized Dodge Charger
ScatPack with Taekwon's license in hand.

At the driver's window - Officer Johnson hands Kisheed the
identification.

                    OFFICER JOHNSON
          Here you go! Everything has checked
          out. Just make sure you keep a
          physical copy of your registration
          in your vehicle at all times.

                    KISHEED
          Yes, sir!

Officer Johnson takes out his cellphone.

                    OFFICER JOHNSON
          Hey Taekwon, if you don't mind. Can
          I get a picture with you before we
          leave?

                    KISHEED
          Aight...

EXT. ADVANCE AUTO PARTS - CONTINUOUS

Kisheed stands directly next to Officer Johnson. Officer
Johnson shoves his cellphone into Officer Gamble's hands.

                    OFFICER JOHNSON
          Jim take the picture.

Kisheed crosses his arms, gives a little smirk. Officer
Johnson throws up the piece sign.

                    OFFICER GAMBLE
          Say Officer Johnson is a groupie!

                    KISHEED
          Officer Johnson is a groupie.

                    OFFICER JOHNSON
          What?

FLASH! Officer Gamble hands the phone back.

                    OFFICER GAMBLE
          Follow me...

<u>ACT TWO</u>

EXT. SAINT MARK'S MISSIONARY BAPTIST CHURCH - NIGHT

A police cruiser drives through the parking lot with its
spot light on. OFFICER CHEN, early 30s, locates Taekwon.

                         TAEKWON
                 Finally!

Taekwon walks toward the police cruiser. Officer Chen's
voice *crackles* through the PA system:

                         PA SYSTEM
                 Stop right there! Don't move, turn
                 around, put your hands up.

Officer Chen exits his vehicle. Pats Taekwon down.

                         OFFICER CHEN
                 Turn around and put your hands
                 down. Now, what's going on?

                         TAEKWON
                 Officer, I was carjacked about
                 twenty minutes ago at the gas
                 station down the street.

                         OFFICER CHEN
                 Let me see some identification.

                         TAEKWON
                 Sorry, I don't have any. I
                 accidentally dropped my wallet when
                 I saw the guy coming towards me. He
                 had on a ski-mask and a gun in his
                 hand.

Officer Chen retrieves a pen and pad.

                         OFFICER CHEN
                 What's your name and social
                 security number?

                         TAEKWON
                 My name is Taekwon Jordan. My
                 social security number is four five
                 three twenty one six four five
                 four.

                    OFFICER CHEN
          For my safety I'm going to handcuff
          you and put you in the back of my
          police cruiser. But listen; you're
          not under arrest. It's normal
          procedure. I want to make sure
          you're story checks out and that
          you don't have any outstanding
          warrants.

                    TAEKWON
          Alright.

Officer Chen handcuffs Taekwon. Pushes him in the police
cruiser.

INT. OFFICER CHEN'S POLICE CRUISER - CONTINUOUS

Officer Chen unhooks a dash mounted radio receiver.

                    OFFICER CHEN
          Dispatch!

                    DISPATCH (O.C.)
          Go Ahead...

                    OFFICER CHEN
          Can you run this social security
          number for me?

Officer Chen reads the note pad.

                    DISPATCH (O.C.)
          That social security number comes
          back to a Taekwon Jordan, black
          male, seventeen.

                    OFFICER CHEN
          Ten - Four!

Officer Gamble chimes in:

                    OFFICER GAMBLE (O.C.)
          We just escorted Taekwon Jordan to
          Norfolk State university about ten
          minutes ago.

                    TAEKWON
          That's impossible. I'm Taekwon! He
          must've used my driver's license.

                    OFFICER CHEN
          Whelp, until we figure everything
          out. You have to come with me.

EXT. NORFOLK STATE UNIVERSITY SPARTAN SUITES - NIGHT

COACH JONES, early 40s, African American, tall, leads
Kisheed into Spartan Suites. They walk past a manned
security desk. Stop in front of an apartment door.

                    COACH JONES
          This is your room right here.

Coach Jones hands Kisheed the key.

                    COACH JONES (cont'd)
          Practice is at six thirty a.m.
          Don't be late!

                    KISHEED
          Coach, am I allowed to leave? You
          know. Maybe go get somethin' to
          eat?

                    COACH JONES
          Absolutely not! You're the first
          top ten basketball recruit to
          commit to NSU in the school's
          history. We're not letting you out
          of our sight.

                    KISHEED
          So what am I gonna do about food?
          I'm starvin'.

                    COACH JONES
          Get it delivered.

Coach Jones pulls a twenty from his wallet.

                    COACH JONES (cont'd)
          Take this... Order some food and
          get some rest. My assistant will be
          here to pick you up first thing in
          the morning.

                    KISHEED
          Aight, thanks!

Coach Jones begins to walk away. Suddenly, he stops and
turns around.

                         COACH JONES
              And one last thing before I leave.
              Don't even think about sneaking out
              because we will see you.

Coach Jones points to a small, almost invisible, circular
object.

                         COACH JONES (cont'd)
              We have cameras everywhere!

INT. NORFOLK STATE SPARTAN SUITES RM 01 - CONTINUOUS

Kisheed enters with cellphone, Customized Dodge Charger
ScatPack keys, in hand.

The apartment door *SLAMS!*

Directly in front are a TV, couch, and coffee table. Off to
the right - A kitchen with an island surrounded by bar
stools. Just pass the kitchen Kisheed notices a WINDOW.

Kisheed quickly walks in that direction, unlocks the lever,
pulls the lift. SEALED! Kisheed walks down a hallway to an
open door. Reaches inside, turns on the light.

INT. NORFOLK STATE SPARTAN SUITES - BEDROOM - CONTINUOUS

In front (2) end tables with lamps surround a king size bed.
A few feet away, another window. Kisheed makes his way over.
Unlocks the lever, pulls the lift. SEALED!

INT. NORFOLK STATE SPARTAN SUITES - LIVING ROOM - CONTINUOUS

Kisheed sits down on the couch. Takes out his cellphone,
dials a number.

INT. CROWN VICTORIA - NIGHT

MUSIC CUE: "I Do This" by Key Glock & Gucci Mane.

Dieuson drives, Katorah rides shotgun, Marquail on the
backseat with his wheel chair folded next to him.

Marquail's cellphone illuminates: SHEED!

                         MARQUAIL
              Ayo, Dieuson turn the radio down.
              It's Sheed.

Dieuson turns the knob on the Sony double din radio.

                    MARQUAIL
          Yurp?

                    KISHEED (O.C.)
          Yo... Who you with?

                    MARQUAIL
          Dieuson and Katorah. Why wassap?

                    KISHEED (O.C.)
          Can they hear me?

                    MARQUAIL
          Nah...

                    KISHEED (O.C.)
          Well put me on speaker.

                    MARQUAIL
          Aight, hold on.

Marquail presses the screen. SPEAKER - PHONE:

                    MARQUAIL (cont'd)
          Aight, Kisheed we can hear you.

                    KISHEED (O.C.)
          Y'all not goin' to believe what
          just happened to me.

          KATORAH   DIEUSON
What?   What?

                    MARQUAIL
          What?

Kisheed laughs.

                    KISHEED (O.C.)
          Yo... Y'all sound like that song by
          OG on drink champs. What, what,
          what, what, what... But anyway,
          after I dropped Marquail off. I
          walked to the corner store. When I
          got there. I saw a guy standin'
          next to a scat. So I took out my
          cellphone to snap a pic, but he
          dropped his wallet and took off
          runnin'.

                    MARQUAIL
          That fuckin' shiesty! He probably
          thought you were tryin' to rob him.

                    KISHEED (O.C.)
          I don't know. But that's not the
          worst part.

                    KATORAH
          Don't tell me you stole the car.

                    KISHEED
              Yesssir!

Dieuson peers into the rear view mirror.

                    DIEUSON
          Aye Kisheed, pull up to the waffle
          house.

                    KISHEED (O.C.)
          I can't! I'm stuck at Norfolk State
          right now.

                    MARQUAIL
          What you doin' at Norfolk state?
          Lookin' for some thots.

INTERCUT WITH:

INT. NORFOLK STATE SPARTAN SUITES - KITCHEN - NIGHT

With cellphone against ear - Kisheed opens the refrigerator,
freezer, microwave, consecutively.

                    KISHEED
          Hell nawl! Right after I drove off.
          I got pulled over by twelve. I gave
          them the driver's license from the
          wallet. But it turned out to be
          Taekwon Jordan. That top ten
          basketball recruit who committed to
          NSU. They gave me a police escort
          here and the basketball coach was
          waiting on me. He led me to this
          apartment and now I'm stuck.

                    KATORAH (O.C.)
          Bro, get out of there!

                    MARQUAIL (O.C.)
              Yeah!

... Kisheed opens the apartment door, peeks out.

INT. NORFOLK STATE SPARTAN SUITES - CONTINUOUS

At the Security Desk - A SECURITY GUARD, late 30s, African American, reading a book, glances at Kisheed. Kisheed quickly closes the door.

                    KISHEED
          I can't! A security guard is right
          outside the room.

                    KATORAH (O.C.)
          What about a window?

                    KISHEED
          They won't open.

                    MARQUAIL (O.C.)
          Now, what you gonna do?

                    KISHEED
          I'm goin' to practice in the
          mornin'. I have to pretend like I'm
          Taekwon until I can get away!

                    MARQUAIL (O.C.)
          I bet you ain't dunkin' on none of
          them college boys.

                    KISHEED
          Bullshit! I'm dunkin' the first
          chance I get. I'm gonna go crazy.
          I'll show the coach what a real top
          ten player looks like.

                    KATORAH (O.C.)
          Honestly, this might be your only
          chance to make it into the league.

                    KISHEED
          Facts! And before I hang up. I got
          a joke for y'all.

Kisheed waits for a response. Silence.

                    KISHEED (cont'd)
          Aight... That's why one of y'all is
          gonna be haunted by an owl.

          MARQUAIL (O.C.)   KATORAH (O.C.)
Who?   Who?

                    DIEUSON (O.C.)
          Who?

Kisheed burst out laughing.

INT. PORTSMOUTH PD - INTERROGATION ROOM - NIGHT

Officer Chen turns on the light. Removes the handcuffs,
pulls out a chair. Taekwon sits down.

                    OFFICER CHEN
          I'll be right back.

INT. PORTSMOUTH PD - SERGEANT SYKES OFFICE - CONTINUOUS

SERGEANT SYKES, late 50s, sits behind a desk. Officer Gamble
stands just inside the doorway.

                    OFFICER GAMBLE
          We escorted a black male, in
          possession of Taekwon's ID and
          vehicle to Norfolk state.

Officer Chen enters. Stands on the opposite side of Officer
Gamble.

                    OFFICER CHEN
          I picked up a black male at Saint
          Mark baptist church and the social
          security number he gave me came
          back to a Taekwon Jordan.

                    SERGEANT SYKES
          Obviously, one of them is an
          imposter. Officer Chen hold on to
          your suspect until we can
          positively identify him.

                    OFFICER CHEN
          Ten - Four!

                    SERGEANT SYKES
          Officer Gamble get in contact with
          Norfolk state police department.
          Brief them on the situation.

                    OFFICER GAMBLE
          Copy that!

INT. PORTSMOUTH PD - INTERROGATION ROOM - NIGHT

Taekwon sleeps on the floor with both arms tucked into his shirt. Officer Chen enters.

                    OFFICER CHEN
          Time to get up.

                    TAEKWON
          Am I good to go?

                    OFFICER CHEN
          No, you have to come with me until
          we can positively identify you.

INT. PORTSMOUTH PD - CONTINUOUS

Taekwon stands in front of a line-up poster. 6'6". FLASH!

                    OFFICER CHEN
          Turn to the left.

FLASH! Taekwon exits. Follows Officer Chen to a fingerprint scanner resting on top of a counter.

                    OFFICER CHEN (cont'd)
          Give me your right hand.

Taekwon follows his instructions. Officer Chen places each individual finger on the scanner.

                    OFFICER CHEN (cont'd)
          This way.

Officer Chen leads Taekwon down a hallway to another room. Opens the door.

INT. PORTSMOUTH PD - NURSE OFFICE - CONTINUOUS

Taekwon sits down at a table. A NURSE, 30s, removes a syringe, vial, and alcohol wipes from a phlebotomy container.

                    NURSE
          Arm, please.

Taekwon extends it. Nurse rubs Taekwon's forearm. Pokes it with a needle until it SWELLS. Officer Chen directs Taekwon to one last location before dropping him off at...

INT. PORTSMOUTH PD - GENERAL POPULATION - CONTINUOUS

Taekwon enters with a mattress under his arm and a small
knit bag containing: Toothpaste, soap, razor, shaving cream
in hand.

The cell door *SLAMS!*

Directly in front are the urinals, sinks, and two
independent showers. Off to the right are a line of INMATES
waiting to use the phone.

OTHER INMATES are sitting on, or around, a table watching
TV. Just pass them are the bunks. Taekwon slowly walks in
that direction.

A voice from a HIDDEN INMATE yells out:

                    HIDDEN INMATE
          Ain't no bunks back here!

Taekwon stops. Rest up against the nearest wall. An OLDER
INMATE, with balding long hair, walks pass with a towel on
his shoulder, soap in hand, bare foot.

Another inmate we'll call TYRONE, late 30s, African
American, bald head, stocky build, jumps off the table and
confronts him.

                    TYRONE
          Hey don't be walkin' on this floor
          with yo naked feet. Put on some
          damn shower shoes!

                    OLDER INMATE
          Sorry about that. I'll go get them
          right now.

Taekwon's POV. Inmates are sleeping everywhere. Everywhere,
except for a empty spot along the wall. Next to the last
urinal.

Taekwon props the mattress on the floor, sits the knit bag
next to it and lays down.

... A TALL INMATE steps in front of the last urinal.
Unfastens his prison jumpsuit. Starts pissing and it
splashes. EVERYWHERE!

INT. WAFFLE HOUSE - NIGHT

Dieuson, Katorah, and Marquail patiently wait for their orders near the entrance.

                              KATORAH
                    It looks like they're about to
                    fight.

                              DIEUSON
                    Yeah.

At the register - An INEBRIATED MAN, early 20s, argues with THE COOK.

                              INEBRIATED MAN
                    DAMN, HOW LONG Y'ALL GONNA TAKE?

                              THE COOK
                    Sir, calm down. We're cooking as
                    fast as we can.

                              INEBRIATED MAN
                    WELL, Y'ALL NEED TO HURRY THE FUCK
                    UP.

                              THE COOK
                    Sir, please don't curse at me.

                              INEBRIATED MAN
                    I CAN CURSE AT WHOEVER THE FUCK I
                    WANT TOO. MOTHERFUCKER!

Inebriated man grabs the napkin dispenser. Chucks it at The Cook. MISSES! The cook comes from around the counter. Swings a wild haymaker that connects. CRACK!

Inebriated Man falls. Unintentionally, knocks Marquail out of his wheelchair.

                              MARQUAIL
                    Bruh, get the fuck up off of me!

Katorah and Dieuson rush to help. Marquail rejects the attempts.

                              MARQUAIL (cont'd)
                    I got it. I can get up! I'm not
                    handicap!

                              KATORAH
                    My bad.

                    DIEUSON
          Say less.

                    MARQUAIL
          I hate this fuckin' wheelchair. All
          over some damn candy.

CARD: 2 YEARS EARLIER

INT. WALMART SUPERCENTER - MORNING

Kisheed and Marquail (wearing Covid-19 mask). Shoplift candy
from a closed checkout register.

                    MARQUAIL
                  (whispers)
          Grab sum candy bars!

                    KISHEED
          Aight, get sum gum.

Marquail with pant legs tucked into his socks. Stuffs gum,
Twizzlers, beef jerky, Mentos, Altoids, Tic Tacs down his
waistband.

Kisheed crams Snickers, Twix, Kit Kats, into his hoodie
front pocket.

INT. WALMART SUPERCENTER - SECURITY OFFICE - CONTINUOUS

Walmart security guard PREVO, early 30s, stocky build, long
dreadlocks, watches the boys on the security camera.

Prevo speaks into a walkie-talkie. Exits the Security
Office. (Hidden between the entrance and small game room).

INT. WALMART SUPERCENTER - CONTINUOUS

Prevo casually walks toward the boys. Kisheed notices...

                    KISHEED
          Oh shit, there go security. RUN!!!

Kisheed sprints towards the exit located at the opposite end
of the store. Marquail slowly trails behind.

EXT. WALMART SUPERCENTER - CONTINUOUS

OFFICER LAWLESS, 30s, quickly exits his police cruiser.
Steps in front of Kisheed. Kisheed stops, changes direction,
bolts pass. Marquail wasn't as lucky.

A struggle pursues...

                    OFFICER LAWLESS
          Stop! Don't move! Stop resisting!

Marquail breaks away. BANG!

Back To Scene

                    MARQUAIL
          Plus that dumb ass cop still out
          here terrorizin' the streets.

EXT. GEORGE WASHINGTON HIGHWAY - NIGHT

A SUSPECT, 20s, African American, with arms handcuffed
behind his back. Sits on a street curb, in between a Police
Cruiser and DARK SEDAN.

Next to him - An UNDERCOVER OFFICER, 30s, body cam attached,
rest a hand on his shoulder. Officer Lawless arrives at the
scene. Makes a BEELINE straight to Suspect.

Body Cam View - KAPOW! Officer Lawless violently punches
Suspect in the face. Suspect squints in pain, leans forward,
and gets up.

Undercover Officer wrestles Suspect back to the ground.
Officer Lawless pins his knee on the back of Suspect's neck.

EXT. JOSEPH G. ECHOLS MEMORIAL HALL - MORNING

Norfolk State's basketball arena, primary athletics facility
and the home for the school's Army Reserve Officer Training
Corps since it opened its doors in November 1982.

The building was named after the late Joseph Echols, who
dedicated more than 20 years to the advancement of
athletics, health and physical education at NSU.

<u>ACT THREE</u>

INT. JOSEPH G. ECHOLS MEMORIAL HALL - CONTINUOUS

Kisheed and NSU MEN'S BASKETBALL TEAM warm up in the gym.
They do lay-ups, shoot three pointers, dunk. Coach Jones
arrives.

                         COACH JONES
                    (yells)
              Taekwon, come here.

Kisheed continues to warm up. PLAYER #1, African American,
early 20s, tall, mumbles.

                         PLAYER #1
              Hey, Taekwon.

Player #1 points at Coach Jones. Kisheed turns around.

                         KISHEED
              Ohhhh...

Kisheed darts over.

                         KISHEED (cont'd)
              You called me Coach?

                         COACH JONES
              Yes, for a second I thought you
              forgot your own name.

                         KISHEED
              Sorry Coach, I couldn't hear you.

                         COACH JONES
              I want you to play point guard in a
              five on five scrimmage with the
              team.

                         KISHEED
              Aight...

INT. MEMORIAL HALL - BASKETBALL COURT - CONTINUOUS

PLAYER #2 takes the ball out of bounds. Passes it to
Kisheed. Kisheed dribbles the ball up the floor.

Stops at the top of the key. Motions for everyone to back
up. Kisheed crosses over PLAYER #3. Steps back. SWISH!

Drains the shot. Kisheed holds up three fingers. Runs back down the court. PLAYER #4 takes the ball out of bounds.

Passes it to Player #1. Player #1 sprints down the court, pass all the other players.

Leaving him and Kisheed all alone. Man to Man. 1 on 1. Player #1 goes in for a two handed dunk.

Kisheed steps in front. Contests the dunk with a ferocious block. SPLAT! The balls soars into the empty bleachers.

Kisheed waives his index finger like "Mutombo."

                         KISHEED
                      (deep voice)
                   No, no, no...

Player #3 climbs the bleachers, locates the ball. Returns court side. Player #3 takes the ball out of bounds.

Passes it to Player #1 who shoots a jumper. BOING! Kisheed catches the rebound.

No-look passes it to Player #2. Who passes it to PLAYER #5. Player #5 dribbles it down the court.

Kisheed sprints to the baseline. Runs around until wide open on the wing. Gestures for the ball.

Player #5 passes it to Kisheed. Kisheed dribbles it once then goes in for the "Anthony Edwards" one handed poster.

Player #1 peeps.

                         PLAYER #1
                   Oh, hell nah.

Kisheed rises higher, slams the ball into Player #1's face. KABOOM! They tangle up in the air.

BOOM! Smash down on the court. Kisheed springs up. Lets out a very LOUD:

                         KISHEED
                   AND ONE!

Player #1 shoves Kisheed.

                         PLAYER #1
                   Watch out!

On the sideline - Coach Jones writes on a notepad. Speaks to a member of the COACHING STAFF.

                    COACH JONES
          This kid is absolutely amazing! I
          don't remember seeing any of this
          on tape.

                    STAFF MEMBER
          Agreed, I guess now we finally see
          what a top ten basketball player
          looks like.

INT. JOSEPH G. ECHOLS MEMORIAL HALL - CONTINUOUS

A side door opens. ASSISTANT, early 20s, African American, female, escorts DETECTIVE TOM PEER, early 50s, sporting a police badge, to Coach Jones.

                    TOM
          Robert Jones?

                    COACH JONES
          Yes.

Tom extends a hand. Coach Jones shakes it.

                    TOM
          How are you doing today? My name is
          Tom Peer and I'm investigating a
          carjacking case. Do you have
          someone here claiming to be Taekwon
          Jordan?

                    COACH JONES
          Yes, he's right there on the court.

Coach Jones points to Kisheed.

                    COACH JONES (cont'd)
          TAEKWON!

Kisheed glances at Coach Jones. Then focuses on the police badge draped on Detective Tom Peer. SKRT! Kisheed takes off running like Taekwon that fateful night.

Kisheed bolts pass Coach Jones, the Detective, and Staff Member. Locates the exit. Burst through the door with a thunderous. BOOM!

EXT. MEMORIAL HALL - PARKING LOT - CONTINUOUS

NORFOLK POLICE SWAT TEAM, in tactical gear, heavily armed,
line the side of the building. NORFOLK STATE POLICE cruisers
block the parking lot exits.

                         SWAT TEAM MEMBER
                Freeze! Don't move!

Kisheed raises his arms in the air. He's tackled to the
ground, handcuffed, and led to a waiting police cruiser.

INT. PORTSMOUTH PD - GENERAL POPULATION - DAY

Taekwon, with the phone receiver against his ear. Dials a
number on the wall mounted phone. Inmate Tyrone walks up
behind. CLICK! Presses the hook.

                         TYRONE
                Phone check, lil nigga!

Taekwon hangs up the receiver.

                         TAEKWON
                I need to make a phone call.

                         TYRONE
                Nah, this my phone. You have to ask
                me before you can use it.

                         TAEKWON
                    (dejected)
                Can I use your phone?

                         TYRONE
                Yeah, if you give me your knit bag.

Reluctantly, Taekwon complies.

INT. DUKE BIRTHING CENTER - DIANA'S OFFICE - DAY

A YOUNG MOTHER, early 20s, relaxes on a medical bed, next to
an Ultrasound screen. DR. DIANA JORDAN, early 50s, wearing a
Smartwatch and AirPod, moves a transducer around on her
abdomen.

Dr. Diana Jordan's cellphone vibrates inside her lab coat
front pocket. She glances at her smartwatch. Then blurts
out:

                    DIANA
          Answer!

                    AIRPOD
          This is a prepaid call from:
          Taekwon. An inmate at the
          Portsmouth city jail.

                    DIANA
                (to Young Mother)
          I have to take this call.

Young Mother nods.

INT. MEMORIAL HALL - COACH JONES OFFICE - DAY

Detective Tom peer sits across a desk from Coach Jones.

                    COACH JONES
          Can you please tell me what's going
          on?

                    TOM
          Sure. I'm currently working a
          carjacking case. Portsmouth police
          detained a young man last night and
          the social security number he gave
          came back to Taekwon Jordan.

                    COACH JONES
          Wait a minute... So you're telling
          me that wasn't Taekwon.

                    TOM
          Yes, that's the reason why he tried
          to get away.

                    COACH JONES
          Are you serious?

                    TOM
          Absolutely! I called you last night
          but you didn't answer. So I left a
          voicemail.

Coach Jones looks at his cellphone.

                    COACH JONES
          I usually put my phone on silent at
          night. So I can get a couple hours
          of sleep before practice.

                    TOM
          I totally understand.

Coach Jones cellphone rings. The screen displays: Taekwon's
Mother.

                    COACH JONES
          Hold on for a second. Here's
          Taekwon's mother calling me now.

Coach Jones holds the phone against his ear.

                    COACH JONES (cont'd)
          OK, I'm on my way now.

Tom removes a business card from his wallet. Hands it to
Coach Jones.

                    TOM
          If you have any other questions.
          Give me a call.

                    COACH JONES
          Thanks, I appreciate it!

INT. PORTSMOUTH MOMMA'S LAUNDRY LAND - DAY

Tifany folds clothes on a table. Cellphone rings, she
answers.

                    KISHEED (O.C.)
          This is a prepaid call from:
          Kisheed... An inmate at the Norf...

Cutoff by:

                    TIFANY
          I'll accept charges.

                    KISHEED (O.C.)
          Ma, I need you to pick me up from
          Norfolk city jail.

                    TIFANY
          Boy, what did you do?

                    KISHEED (O.C.)
          I didn't do nothin'.

                    TIFANY
          Then why do you need me?

                    KISHEED
          Because I'm a minor.

Tifany exhales.

                    TIFANY
          Damn, I'm on my way.

INT. NORFOLK PD - INTERROGATION ROOM - NIGHT

Tifany and Kisheed sit across a table from Detective Tom
Peer.

                    TOM
          Your son is being charged with
          carjacking and criminal
          impersonation.

Furious, Kisheed snaps at Detective Tom Peer.

                    KISHEED
          I DIDN'T CARJACK NOBODY!

Kisheed turns to Tifany.

                    KISHEED (cont'd)
          Ma, I saw a guy standin' next to a
          car at the corner store. So, I
          pulled out my phone to take a
          picture. But for some strange
          reason he dropped his wallet and
          took off runnin'. I waited to see
          if he was gonna come back but he
          never did. So, I took the car for a
          joyride.

Tom writes down the testimony.

                    TOM
          Taking someone's car without their
          permission is against the law. But,
          in light of this new evidence I
          need to speak to my superior.

Tom leaves. Tifany slaps Kisheed on the back of the head.

                    TIFANY
          Boy, what the fuck is wrong with
          you?

                    KISHEED
          Ouch! I'm sorry ma.

Tifany slaps him again.

INT. PORTSMOUTH PD - INMATE PROCESSING - NIGHT

Coach Jones, standing near the exit, observes the continuous
activity of "Inmate Processing." First, a BELLIGERENT DRUNK
walks pass mumbling to himself.

Next, a WOMAN of the night trying to fix a wig. And
finally...

                    TAEKWON
          Coach, am I glad to see you.

Taekwon hugs Coach Jones. Coach Jones pats him on the back.

                    COACH JONES
          Are you OK?

                    TAEKWON
          Yes, I'm fine.

Coach Jones catches a whiff of Taekwon!

                    COACH JONES
          Are you sure?

                    TAEKWON
          Yes, why coach?

                    COACH JONES
          Because it smells like someone peed
          them self.

                    TAEKWON
          NO! I had to sleep on the floor
          next to a toilet.

                    COACH JONES
          OK, lets go.

EXT. PORTSMOUTH PD - PARKING LOT - CONTINUOUS

Coach Jones leads Taekwon to a Norfolk State University
wrapped passenger van.

                    TAEKWON
          Hey coach, do you know what
          happened to my car?

                    COACH JONES
          It still should be parked at
          spartan suites because I know for a
          fact the kid didn't leave.

INT. NORFOLK STATE UNIVERSITY VAN - CONTINUOUS

                    TAEKWON
          What happened to him?

                    COACH JONES
          He was arrested this morning after
          practice.

Taekwon scowls at Coach Jones.

                    TAEKWON
          After practice? Come on Coach, you
          couldn't tell that wasn't me?

                    COACH JONES
          Honestly, I couldn't. You two look
          alike. And at practice I wasn't
          focused on how he looked. I was
          more focused on how he played.

Taekwon gives Coach Jones a troubled look.

INT. NORFOLK PD - INTERROGATION ROOM - NIGHT

Kisheed sleeps, head down on the table. Tifany plays Candy
Crush on her cellphone. Tom enters.

                    TIFANY
          About time! I'm ready to go.

                    TOM
          You're free to go Ms. Savage. But
          your son has to stay at the
          juvenile detention center until he
          talks to the magistrate.

                    TIFANY
          What time is that?

                    TOM
          Nine a.m.

Tifany nudges Kisheed.

                    TIFANY
          Boy wake up I'm about to leave.
          I'll be back in the morning.

Kisheed sits up in the chair.

                    KISHEED
          What about me?

                    TOM
          This way...

INT. NJDC - INMATE PROCESSING - CONTINUOUS

A series of events in FAST FORWARD! Kisheed processed
exactly the same as Taekwon.

EXT. NSU SPARTAN SUITES - PARKING LOT - NIGHT

Coach Jones parks next to the Customized Dodge Charger
ScatPack.

                    TAEKWON
          Do you have the keys?

                    COACH JONES
          No, but you can check and see if
          it's unlocked. The keys might be
          inside.

Taekwon gets out, pulls the door handle. LOCKED!

                    TAEKWON
          Dang!

... Coach Jones and Taekwon enter spartan suites. Stop in
front of apartment 01.

                    COACH JONES
          OK, lets try this again.

Coach Jones opens the door.

INT. NORFOLK STATE SPARTAN SUITES RM 01 - CONTINUOUS

A pillow with a bundled up sheet rest on the couch. An empty
pizza box and drink are on the table. Coach Jones and
Taekwon thoroughly inspect the apartment.

                    COACH JONES
          Other then this trash, everything
          else looks in order.

                    TAEKWON
          But I didn't find my car keys.

Coach Jones picks up the bundled up sheet. *Shakes* it. A set
of KEYS fall out.

                    TAEKWON (cont'd)
          There they are!

                    COACH JONES
          Good!

Coach Jones gathers the trash.

                    COACH JONES (cont'd)
          I have to go. Get some rest. My
          assistant will be here in the
          morning to pick you up.

                    TAEKWON
          Six thirty right?

                    COACH JONES
          That's right!

INT. MEMORIAL HALL - BASKETBALL COURT - MORNING

Taekwon misses open shots, gets the ball stolen, and loses
it out of bounds. He goes up for a dunk. SLAT! Player #1
blocks it.

                    PLAYER #1
          Get that weak shit outta here!

                    TAEKWON
          Foul!

Player #1 points an open hand towards the ground.

                    PLAYER #1
          You too little!

Coach Jones blows a whistle.

                    COACH JONES
          Time out!

Coach Jones walks on the court.

                    COACH JONES (cont'd)
          What's wrong Taekwon?

                         TAEKWON
          I don't know coach. My mind is not
          in the game right now.

                         COACH JONES
          OK, have a seat.

Taekwon walks off the court. Sits down on the bench.

INT. MEMORIAL HALL - BASKETBALL COURT - CONTINUOUS

Player #1 whispers to the other players.

                         PLAYER #1
          Top ten is a bust!

The team laughs.

INT. NJDC - MAGISTRATE OFFICE - DAY

Kisheed and Tifany stand in front of a wall mounted TV.

On TV Screen: MAGISTRATE, late 40s, African American,
female, sits behind a desk.

                         MAGISTRATE
          You are charged with grand larceny,
          a felony offense punishable by up
          to twenty years in prison and
          unlawful use of an ID card, a class
          one misdemeanor punishable by up to
          a year in jail. But since this is
          only your first offense and you are
          a minor. The judge is going to
          change the larceny charge to
          joyriding and dismiss the ID
          charge. Your new court date is four
          weeks from now. In that time you
          need to seek legal representation.
          If you cannot afford legal
          representation you can request it
          once this meeting has adjourned.

<u>ACT FOUR</u>

INT. MEMORIAL HALL - COACH JONES OFFICE - DAY

Coach Jones sits at his desk with a business card in hand. A
closer look REVEALS: Tom Peer. Detective Norfolk Police
Department. (757) 555-8000.

Taekwon enters.

                    COACH JONES
          What can I do for you Taekwon?

Taekwon takes a deep breath.

                    TAEKWON
          I don't want to play for Norfolk
          state anymore.

                    COACH JONES
          Why what's wrong, Taekwon?

                    TAEKWON
          I've had nothing but bad luck since
          I've been here. I've been
          carjacked, thrown in jail, and the
          other players are calling me a
          bust.

                    COACH JONES
          Taekwon, don't sweat those guys.
          They're just jealous. You're the
          best thing to happen to NSU in
          years.

                    TAEKWON
          It sure doesn't feel like it.

                    COACH JONES.
          I tell you what. Take a few days
          off. Check out the campus. Watch
          and see how much love you will get.
          Trust me you'll be surprise.

Taekwon thinks for a minute.

                    TAEKWON
          Alright, I'll take a few days off
          and see if it's true.

Taekwon leaves. Coach Jones picks up his cellphone, dials
the number.

                    TOM (O.C.)
          Detective Tom Peer. How may I help
          you?

                    COACH JONES
          Tom, this is Robert, Norfolk state
          men's basketball coach. I have a
          question for you.

                    TOM (O.C.)
          I'm listening.

                    COACH JONES
          Did you ever find out that kids
          name from Taekwon Jordan's
          carjacking case?

                    TOM (O.C.)
          Yes, I did. But unfortunately he's
          a minor. So I won't be able to give
          you that information.

                    COACH JONES
          I understand. Thanks anyway.

INT. DALE HOME'S APARTMENT - KISHEED'S BEDROOM - NIGHT

Kisheed sits in front of the 3D printer. Removes a custom
made Glock-17 pistol frame. Tifany walks pass, opens the
front door. Kisheed follows.

                    KISHEED
          Ma, where you goin'?

                    TIFANY
          To work, why?

                    KISHEED
          I'm hungry. Can I go with you?

                    TIFANY
          Yeah boy, come on!

INT. COCK ISLAND BAR AND GRILL - NIGHT

Tifany makes drinks for the customers. "Jack and Coke", "Gin
and Dubonnet." She washes out glasses. Wipes down the bar.

Table off to the side - Kisheed Devours hot wings. Tifany
makes her way over.

                    TIFANY
          You good?

                    KISHEED
          Yeah, ma.

Kisheed wipes his fingers with a napkin. Pulls out his
cellphone, dials a number.

INT. RAP STUDIO - BOOTH - NIGHT

Dieuson, wearing headphones, stands in front of a filtered
microphone with cellphone in hand.

Dieuson's cellphone illuminates - "Kisheed."

EXT. RAP STUDIO - CONTINUOUS

Dieuson sits down in the Crown Victoria.

                    DIEUSON
          What's up Kisheed? Where you at?

                    KISHEED (O.C.)
          Cock Island.

                    DIEUSON
          Say less.

INT. COCK ISLAND BAR AND GRILL - MOMENTS LATER

Dieuson enters. Tifany glances at Dieuson with an evil look.
Eventually, she points to the table off to the side.

                    DIEUSON
          Wassap Kisheed?

                    KISHEED
          Sup, my boy. You tryin' to play
          some pool?

                    DIEUSON
          No doubt!

At the Pool Table - Kisheed slides quarters into the slot,
removes the balls, and racks them. Dieuson grabs a pool
stick. Rubs some chalk on the end.

Aims -- CRACK! The balls scatter.

                         DIEUSON (cont'd)
               I'm about to run the table on yo
               ass.

                         KISHEED
               That's cap!

... A BAR PATRON, Caucasian, 20s, bumps into Dieuson.
Dieuson misses the shot.

                         DIEUSON
               Yo, watch where the fuck you goin'!

Bar Patron turns around. Speaks in an AGGRESSIVE tone.

                         BAR PATRON
               What did you say?

Dieuson puts the pool stick down. Gets up into Bar Patron's
face. Talks to him as if he doesn't comprehend english.

                         DIEUSON
               Watch... where... the... fuck...
               you... are... goin'... before I
               fuck you up in here!

Kisheed grabs Dieuson by the arm.

                         KISHEED
               Chill, my boy.

Bar Patron backs up. Puts his hands in the air.

                         BAR PATRON
               You got it!

Bar Patron leaves. Dieuson picks up the pool stick.

                         DIEUSON
               Where was I?

                         KISHEED
               You was goin' for the two.

INT. NORFOLK STATE SPARTAN SUITES - BEDROOM - NIGHT

Taekwon's cellphone screen lightens the room as he lays
across the bed. He talks on a Face-Time call with AERIAL,
18, slim, long eyelashes, ponytail with baby hair.

Cellphone Screen: Aerial rest in bed.

                    AERIAL
          Where have you been? I've been
          callin' you.

                    TAEKWON
          I didn't have my phone because I
          was in jail.

                    AERIAL
          Really? What happened?

                    TAEKWON
          I don't want to talk about it right
          now. I'm happy it's all over. But
          now, I'm thinking about de-
          committing from Norfolk state.

                    AERIAL
          Why?

                    TAEKWON
          Because, I've been through a lot
          since I've been here. I honestly
          think it's a sign.

                    AERIAL
          Taekwon, don't forget the real
          reason why you're there.

Taekwon sighs.

                    TAEKWON
          You're absolutely right.

                    AERIAL
          Anyway, so when can I come see you?
          I miss you already.

                    TAEKWON
          First, let me get situated. I
          literally just made it to the
          campus.

                    AERIAL
          Hey Bae, don't be up there
          entertainin' another bitch.

                    TAEKWON
          Aerial!

INT. COCK ISLAND BAR AND GRILL - NIGHT

Dieuson places his pool stick into a holder mounted to the
back wall. Kisheed shoves the triangle rack into the pool
table. Dieuson exits. Kisheed stops by the bar.

                    KISHEED
          Ma, we about to go.

                    TIFANY
          Go straight home!

                    KISHEED
          Aight...

EXT. COCK ISLAND BAR AND GRILL - CONTINUOUS

Dieuson presses a button on a Key FOB. Opens the driver's
door of the Crown Victoria. Parked directly in front of the
side entrance.

OUT OF NOWHERE - Bar Patron emerges, holding a pistol with
an extendo clip in hand.

                    BAR PATRON
          Talk that shit now...

BANG! BANG! BANG! BANG! BANG! BANG!!! Bullets punch through
Dieuson, the Crown Victoria. Shattering the driver's window.
... Kisheed rushes out. Cradles Dieuson in his arms.

                    KISHEED
          Breathe Dieuson.

INT. BYRD & BALDWIN BROS STEAKHOUSE - NIGHT

Fancy. Romantic. Are just a few words to describe Byrd &
Baldwin Bros Steakhouse.

In a small booth - Magistrate and Coach Jones eat dinner.

                    MAGISTRATE
          Really Robert? The most expensive
          restaurant in Norfolk?

Coach Jones smiles.

                    COACH JONES
          Only the best for you.

                    MAGISTRATE
          Mmm-hmm. What can I do for you?

                    COACH JONES
          I'm looking for a juvenile. Charged
          with carjacking and criminal
          impersonation.

EXT. BON SECOURS MARYVIEW MEDICAL CENTER - MORNING

Kisheed paces back and forward in front of the hospital
emergency entrance. A NISSAN ALTIMA pulls into the parking
lot. HONKS the horn. Kisheed gets inside.

INT. NISSAN ALTIMA - CONTINUOUS

                    TIFANY
          Is he gonna make it?

                    KISHEED
          I don't know.

                    TIFANY
          I'm praying for his family and
          Katorah.

Kisheed gazes at Tifany with a puzzled look.

                    KISHEED
          Katorah?

Tifany hands him the Dorian Finney-Smith Jersey.

                    TIFANY
          Here, this was all I could find.

Kisheed pulls it on.

                    KISHEED
          Ewww, what are all these stains on
          my shirt?

Tifany frowns.

                    TIFANY
          Katorah and Dieuson.

INT. WNSB HOT 91.1 FM - DAY

A neon, "Hot tea and Incense" sign, hangs on the wall of a large office. Known as - THE SOUL OF VA.

Below the sign - Taekwon sits at a table across from MICHAEL, early 30s, African American, in front of Pod-cast microphones, with tea cups and incense burning.

                    MICHAEL
          Taekwon Jordan. How are you doing
          today?

                    TAEKWON
          I'm good, thanks.

                    MICHAEL
          You're welcome. OK, lets get
          straight to it. Why did you choose
          Norfolk state?

                    TAEKWON
          I chose Norfolk state because I'm
          looking for my long lost identical
          twin brother. We never met, but
          were born here in Virginia. My
          biological mom had us at sixteen
          and wanted to give us up for
          adoption. But the doctor, my
          adoptive mom, convinced her to keep
          him, while she took care of me,
          until I finished high school.

                    MICHAEL
          That's a fascinating story. Do you
          know your brother's name?

                    TAEKWON
          No, but my father's name is Rasheed
          Watson. And if anyone listening
          knows where he is or where I can
          find him. Please contact the
          athletic department here at Norfolk
          State University.

INT. PORTSMOUTH PD SERGEANT SYKES OFFICE - DAY

Sergeant Sykes stares at his desktop computer screen. Officer Lawless knocks on the open door.

                    OFFICER LAWLESS
          You wanted to see me?

                    SERGEANT SYKES
          Yes, come on in and have a seat.

Sergeant Sykes turns the desktop computer screen around.
Presses play on a video he has cued up.

<u>On Computer Screen</u>: Officer Lawless strikes Suspect.

                    SERGEANT SYKES (cont'd)
               Explain...

Officer Lawless doesn't respond.

                    SERGEANT SYKES (cont'd)
               Brian, we hired you to protect and
               serve. Not to assault and batter.
               And unfortunately I have no choice
               but to suspend you without pay
               until we conduct a thorough
               investigation.

INT. DALE HOMES APARTMENTS - BATHROOM - DAY

Blood washes down the drain as Kisheed stands under the
shower sprocket.

INT. DALE HOMES APARTMENTS - LIVING ROOM - CONTINUOUS

Tifany watches TV on the couch. KNOCK! KNOCK! KNOCK!

                    TIFANY
               Who is it?

                    COACH JONES (O.S.)
               Robert Jones, men's basketball
               coach at Norfolk state.

Tifany opens the door.

                    COACH JONES
               Sorry to bother you. I'm looking
               for the parents of Kisheed Watson.

                    TIFANY
               I'm his mother.

                    COACH JONES
               Is he home?

                    TIFANY
          Yes, he's taking a shower right
          now. One of his friends was shot
          last night.

                    COACH JONES
          I'm so sorry to hear that. But is
          there anyway I can come inside and
          talk to you guys about him possibly
          playing for the team?

                    TIFANY
          Hold on...

INT. DALE HOME'S APARTMENT - LIVING ROOM - MOMENTS LATER

Coach Jones sits on a foldable chair directly in front of
Kisheed.

                    COACH JONES
          Do you always wear a Ski-mask?

                    TIFANY
          Yes, he thinks he's a rapper named
          Pooh Shiesty.

Coach Jones laughs.

                    KISHEED
          No I don't!

                    COACH JONES
          Moving on... Kisheed how come I've
          never heard of you? Did you play
          basketball in high school?

                    KISHEED
          Yeah, but I was cut my sophomore
          year. The coach said I wasn't a
          team player.

                    COACH JONES
          Are you in school now?

                    KISHEED
          No, I'm supposed to be a senior but
          I stopped goin' after summer break.

                    COACH JONES
          Oh, how were your grades?

                    KISHEED
          I was on the honor roll.

                    COACH JONES
          Nice. OK, I have a personal
          question to ask you. But listen you
          don't have to answer if you don't
          want too. But just so you know. If
          you have any plans of playing
          basketball at the next level. It
          will have to be made public.

                    KISHEED
          Aight...

                    COACH JONES
          Do you have any felonies?

Kisheed thinks for a moment.

                    KISHEED
          No.

                    TIFANY
          Kisheed!

                    KISHEED
          Wait, that joyridin' case might be
          a felony.

                    COACH JONES
          That's right! Leaving you with only
          two options. Option number one. Go
          back to school, get your diploma,
          and I promise you a full ride
          scholarship at Norfolk State. Or
          option number two. Go to jail and
          have a felony on you're record.

Kisheed extends a hand.

                    KISHEED
          Promise?

Coach Jones shakes it.

                    COACH JONES
          Promise!

                                        FADE OUT